JUST A GIRL

WHO LOVES

COWS

THIS JOURNAL BELONGS TO

JUST A GIRL WHO LOVES COWS

JUST A GIRL WHO LOVES COWS

JUST A GIRL WHO LOVES COWS

JUST A GIRL WHO LOVES COWS

JUST A GIRL
WHO LOVES
COWS

JUST A GIRL WHO LOVES COWS

JUST A GIRL WHO LOVES COWS

Printed in Great Britain
by Amazon